D1013327

Published simultaneously in 1995 by Exley Publications in Great Britain,
and Exley Giftbooks in the USA.

12 11 10 9 8 7 6 5

ISBN 1-85015-642-5

A copy of the CIP data is available from the British Library on request. All rights
reserved. No part of this publication may be reproduced or transmitted in any form or by
any means, electronic or mechanical, including photocopy, recording or any information
in writing from the Publisher.

Edited and pictures selected by Helen Exley.
Pictures researched by Image Select International.
Typesetting by Delta, Watford.
Printed in China.

Exley Publications Ltd, 16 Chalk Hill, Watford, Herts WDl 4BN, United Kingdom.
Exley Publications LLC, 232 Madison Avenue, Suite 1206, New York, NY 10016, USA.

Acknowledgements: The publishers are grateful for permission to reproduce copyright material.
While every effort has been made to trace copyright holders, the publishers would be pleased to
hear from any not here acknowledged.
Pearl Buck: extract from "The Joy Of Children" published by The John Day Co. Inc, New York;
Bill Cosby: extract from "Fatherhood" © 1986 by William H.Cosby Jr. Reprinted by permission of
DoublPday, a division of Bantam Doubleday Dell Publishing Group Inc.; Dan Greenberg: extract
from "Confessions Of A Pregnant Father" © 1986 by Dan Greenberg. Reprinted by permission of
Macmillan Publishing Company/Simon and Schuster; Lewis Grizzard: extracts from "My Daddy
Was A Pistol And I'm The Son Of A Gun" © 1986 by Lewis Grizzard. Reprinted by permission of
Villard Books, a division of Random House Inc.; Edgar Guest: extract from "Moments With
Father" published by Hallmark 1974; Christopher Morley: extract from "Mince Pie" © 1919 by
Christopher Morley. Copyright renewed 1947 by Christopher Morley. Reprinted by permission of
HarperCollins Publishers Inc; Richard Taylor: extract from The New York Times © 1987 by The
New York Times Company. Reprinted with permission; Jon Stewart: extract from "The San
Francisco Examiner" 15 June 1986 © The San Francisco Examiner.
Picture Credits: Exley Publications is very grateful to the following individuals and organizations
for permission to reproduce their pictures: Alinari Archive (AA), Archiv Für Kunst (AKG), The
Bridgeman Art Library (BAL), Edimedia (EDM), Fine Art Photographic Library Ltd (FAP),
Giraudon (GIR), Scala (SCA), Statens Konstmuseer (SKM) Cover: Veronese (SCA); title page: P.
Nomellini (AA); page 6: Silvester Cedrin (SCA); page 8: © 1995 Leonid Ossipowitsch Pasternak
(1862-1945) "The Evening Before the Exam", Musée d'Orsay, Paris (AKG); page 11: P. Nomellini
(AA); page 13: Sir Hubert Von Herkomer (FAP); page 14: © 1995 Robert Gemmell Hutchison
(1855-1936) "Sleep", City of Edinburgh Museums and Art Galleries (BAL); page 17: Delacroix
(EDM); page 19: Giuseppe Moricci (SCA); page 20/21: Stanhope Forbes (EDM); page 23: Frederick
Walker, British Museum, London (BAL); page 24: Pietro Fragiacomo (EDM); page 27: Theophile-
Emmanuel Duverger, Guildhall Art Gallery (BAL); page 28: © 1995 Boris Maluyev (b.1929) "The
First to War", Roy Miles Galery (BAL); page 31: Wladimir Alexandrowitsch Serow (AKG); page
33: Bartolome Esteban Murillo (AKG); page 34: Paul Gauguin (EDM); page 36: © 1995 Willi
Balendat (1901-1969) "Fairground Spectators", Klaus Balendat Collection, Rangendingen (AKG);
page 38/39: P. Nomellini (AA); page 41: B.S. Ugarov (SKM); page 43: Edgar Degas (EDM); page 44:
© 1995 Alvar Jansson "Sondagskladd Family" (SKM); page 46: James Jacques Tissot (GIR); page
49: ©1995 Gareth Lloyd Ball "Twickenham: The Pilkington Cup Final, 1992", Private Collection
(BAL); page 50: © 1995 Gertrude Halsband (1917-1981) "Nature Walk", Private Collection (BAL);
page 53: James Jacques Tissot, Musée des Beaux-Arts (GIR/BAL); page 54: © 1995 William H.
Johnson (1901-1970) Untitled, National Museum of American Art (BAL); page 56/57: Niccolo
Cannicci (SCA); page 58: (AKG); page 61: Helen Allingham (EDM).

Fathers
and
Sons

A HELEN EXLEY GIFTBOOK

EXLEY
NEW YORK • WATFORD, UK

"A boy is a magical creature
– you can lock him out of your
workshop, but you can't lock him
out of your heart."

ALAN BECK

"I do not love him because
he is good, but because he is
my little child."

RABINDRANATH TAGORE (1861-1941)

"It is not flesh and blood but
the heart which makes us
fathers and sons."

SCHILLER (1759-1805)

*"Dad, when you come home at night
with only shattered pieces of your
dreams, your little one
can mend them like new with two magic
words – 'Hi Dad!'"*

ALAN BECK

"To a young boy, the father is a giant from whose shoulders you can see forever."

PERRY GARFINKEL

"Father: Someone we can look up to no matter how tall we get."

ANONYMOUS

"What do I owe my father? Everything."

HENRY VAN DYKE (1852-1933)

"He wants to live on through something – and in his case, his masterpiece is his son ... all of us want that, and it gets more poignant as we get more anonymous in this world."

ARTHUR MILLER, b.1915

"I had heard all those things about fatherhood, how great it is. But it's greater than I'd ever expected – I had no idea Quinton would steal my heart the way he has. From the minute I laid eyes on him, I knew nobody could ever wrestle him away from me."

BURT REYNOLDS, b.1936

"When one becomes a father, then first one becomes a son. Standing by the crib of one's own baby, with that world-old pang of compassion and protectiveness toward this so little creature that has all its course to run, the heart flies back in yearning and gratitude to those who felt just so towards one's self. Then for the first time one understands the homely succession of sacrifices and pains by which life is transmitted and fostered down the stumbling generations."

**CHRISTOPHER MORLEY (1890-1957),
FROM "MINCE PIE"**

"Last night my child was born – a very strong boy, with large black eyes. If you ever become a father, I think the strangest and strongest sensation of your life will be hearing for the first time the thin cry of your own child. For a moment you have the strange feeling of being double; but there is something more, quite impossible to analyze – perhaps the echo in a man's heart of all the sensations felt by all the fathers and mothers of his race at a similar instant in the past. It is a very tender, but also a very ghostly feeling."

**LAFCADIO HEARN (1850-1904),
FROM "THE LETTERS OF LAFCADIO HEARN"**

"Children are a kind of confirmation of life. The only form of immortality that we can be sure of."

PETER USTINOV, b.1921

"Nothing I've ever done has given me more joys and rewards than being a father to my children."

BILL COSBY

"The night you were born I ceased being my father's boy and became my son's father. That night I began a new life."

HENRY GREGOR FELSON

"We never know the love of the parent until we become parents ourselves."

HENRY WARD BEECHER (1813-1887)

"Children's children are the crown
of old men, and the glory of
children is their father."

PROVERBS 17:6

"Some of my memories are nearly forty years old, but they are indelible and they are a comfort. To love someone unconditionally – as I loved Daddy – is to remember each detail of their personage, to remember isolated and long-past moments together, to remember nuances that made such an object of love unique and impossible to replace. That is why I remember, and cherish, the memories of the man's hair, his smell, his likes and dislikes, and his idiosyncrasies."

LEWIS GRIZZARD, FROM "MY DADDY WAS A PISTOL AND I'M A SON OF A GUN"

"When a father sets out to teach his little son to walk, he stands in front of him and holds his two hands on either side of the child, so that he cannot fall, and the boy goes toward his father between his father's hands. But the moment he is close to his father, he moves away a little and holds his hands farther apart, and he does this over and over, so that the child may learn to walk."

THE BAAL SHEM

"Dad, your little boy is your captor, your jailer, your boss and your master – a freckle-faced, pint-sized, cat-chasing bundle of noise."

ALAN BECK

"How easily a father's tenderness is recalled and how quickly a son's offences vanish at the slightest word of repentance!"

MOLIÈRE (1622-1673)

"It's a wonderful feeling when your father becomes not a god but a man to you – when he comes down from the mountain and you see he's this man with weaknesses.
And you love him as this whole being, not as a figurehead."

ROBIN WILLIAMS

"I watched a small man with thick calluses on both hands work fifteen and sixteen hours a day. I saw him once literally bleed from the bottoms of his feet, a man who came here uneducated, alone, unable to speak the language, who taught me all I needed to know about faith and hard work by the simple eloquence of his example."

MARIO CUOMO

"Psychologists have written much about the need to be loved. Less has been said about the need to love. Your love becomes overwhelming when its object is helpless and dependent and your own hold on life seems uncertain. Perhaps Plato was right when he said that our love for our children springs from the soul's yearning for immortality.
I lower my sleeping son into his crib. The Chopin record will shut off automatically after a while, and the house will be still until the baby's first importunate cry in the morning. One more precious, irreplaceable day is ending, and I am fulfilled."

RICHARD TAYLOR, FROM
THE "NEW YORK TIMES", MARCH 29, 1987

"I might have a sex change operation and become a nun, but outside of that I do not think my life could possibly have changed more than it did by becoming a father.
And when my son looks up at me and breaks into his wonderful toothless smile, my eyes fill up and I know that having him is the best thing I will ever do."

DAN GREENBERG, FROM
"CONFESSIONS OF A PREGNANT FATHER"

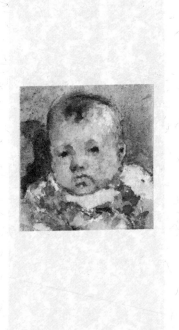

"Once Knute playfully demanded of one of the boys an account of his age. He answered, 'Seven.' 'Impossible,' his father said; 'no young man could possibly get quite so dirty in seven years.' Then he tried to placate the boy's mother with a grotesquely penitential look."

BONNIE ROCKNE, FROM A NOTE IN HER HUSBAND'S AUTOBIOGRAPHY

"What is equally maddening about the visit of your child to some distant home is the call you get from the mother or father there telling you how lovely and helpful your child has been.
'I just can't tell you what a polite young gentleman he is,' the mother says. 'He straightened his room and he made his bed and he·even offered to do the dishes.' At moments like these, you truly feel that you have fallen down the rabbit hole."

BILL COSBY, FROM "FATHERHOOD"

"You heard it said that fathers want their sons to be what they feel they cannot themselves be, but I tell you it also works the other way. A boy wants something very special from his father."

SHERWOOD ANDERSON (1876-1941)

"Parents repeat their lives in their offspring; and their esteem for them is so great, that they feel their sufferings and taste their enjoyments as much as if they were their own."

RAY PALMER

"No man is really depraved who can spend half an hour by himself on the floor playing with his little boy's electric train."

SIMEON STRUNSKY

"The child had every toy his father wanted."

ROBERT E. WHITTEN

"If you've never seen a real, fully developed look of disgust, just tell your son how you conducted yourself when you were a boy."

KIN HUBBARD
[ABE MARTIN ON THINGS IN GENERAL]

"In every dispute between parent and child, both cannot be right, but they may be, and usually are, both wrong. It is this situation which gives family life its peculiar hysterical charm."

ISAAC ROSENFELD

"He makes fuzz come out of my bald patch!"

CHARLES A. LINDBERGH (1902-1974),
ABOUT HIS SON

"Heredity is what a man believes in until his son begins to behave like a delinquent."

PRESBYTERIAN LIFE

"It never occurs to a boy that he will some day be as dumb as his father."

DR. LAURENCE J. PETER

"When I was a boy of fourteen, my father was so ignorant I could hardly stand to have the old man around. But when I got to be twenty-one, I was astounded at how much the old man had learned in seven years."

MARK TWAIN (1835-1910)

Children aren't happy with
nothing to ignore
And that's what parents were
created for.

OGDEN NASH (1902-1971)

"One of the nicest things about being a father is that you don't have to stop being a son. In fact, there's no way around it. Fathers are sons – both subject and predicate, enjoying a privileged two-in-oneness. The fortunate father/son can draw sustenance from two directions – wisdom, strength, and compassion from his own father, and insight and joy from his sons. The child may be father of the man, but if you look closely into your own son's eyes, you'll probably see your father staring back at you."

JON STEWART, FROM "THE SAN FRANCISCO EXAMINER", JUNE 15, 1986

"The essential skill of parenting is making up answers. When an experienced father is driving down the road and his kid asks him how much a certain building weighs, he doesn't hesitate for a second. 'Three thousand, four hundred and fifty-seven tons,' he says."

DAVE BARRY

"The trouble with dads who know the facts is that they don't seem the same facts the teacher knows."

PAM BROWN, b.1928

"Fathers should not get too discouraged
if their sons reject their advice. It will
not be wasted; years later the sons will
offer it to their own offspring."
ANONYMOUS

"The children despise their parents until the
age of forty, when they suddenly become
just like them – thus preserving the system."
QUENTIN CREWE

"Raising kids is part joy and part
guerilla warfare."
ED ASNER

"Safe, for a child, is his father's hand, holding him tight."

PAM BROWN, b.1928

"My dad was always there for me and my brother, and I want my kids to have the same kind of dad – a dad they will remember. Being a dad is the most important thing in my life."

KEVIN COSTNER

"Many an excellent man is tempted to forget that the best offering he can make to his children is himself."

HENRY NEUMANN

"I talk and talk and talk, and I haven't taught people in fifty years what my father taught by example in one week."

MARIO CUOMO

"…your father is a great man whether or not he's a worldly success. He's someone you can look up to. He helps shape your worldview, dispenses discipline, teaches object lessons, hands down material and moral legacies."

JOHN WINOKUR, FROM "FATHERS"

"A happy childhood can't be cured.
Mine'll hang around my neck
like a rainbow, that's all,
instead of a noose."

ANONYMOUS

"The memory of Papa – tall,
dark-haired, with a neatly trimmed
mustache, smiling, warm andloving – is
still vivid in my mind.
It will never fade."

LEO BUSCAGLIA

"The individual human cycle is not whole until man and woman look back to the parents who gave them life and forward to the children to whom they themselves give life. Only thus does the individual feel assured of his place in the eternal scheme of creation. Only thus does his heart find rest."

PEARL BUCK (1892-1973),
FROM "THE JOY OF CHILDREN"

"The need for a father is as crucial as the need for a son, and the search of each for the other – through all the days of one's life – exempts no one. Happy the man who finds both."

MAX LERNER, b.1902

"I knew he was as fine a dad as any boy ever had – kind, cheerful, humorous, hard-working and patient; severe at times over my indifferent effort and boyish carelessness, but severe always with a kindly purpose, and very proud of his children whenever they did anything which seemed worthy. What I didn't know until too late was the depth of his wisdom and the magnitude of his sacrifice."

EDGAR A. GUEST